CHRISTOPHER COLUMBUS

TWO YOUNG BOYS SAT HIGH ABOVE THE SEA

CHRISTOPHER COLUMBUS

Sam Wellman

Illustrated by
Ken Save

ISBN 1-55748-704-9

Published by Barbour Publishing, Inc., P.O. Box 719, Uhrichsville, Ohio 44683 http://www.barbourbooks.com

Printed in the United States of America.

CHAPTER 1

Two young boys sat high above the sea, dangling their legs off a rock wall. They ate lunch there every day so they could watch the ships sail in and out of the harbor. Both boys were tall and red-headed. Freckles covered their long, thin faces. Anyone would know they were brothers.

The older one pointed with a chunk of bread. "Look, Bart. That caravel sailing into the harbor is running the flag of France up its mast!"

"And, look there, Chris, at that galleon unloading its cargo at the docks," answered the boy named Bart, as well as he could while chewing a mouthful of cheese. "It flies the flag of Spain!"

Anyone listening to the brothers Chris and Bart would soon realize there was no flag they could not identify. There was no kind of sea-going ship they did not recognize. They lived in the seaport city of

Genoa in Italy. The sight of seeing sailing ships every day seemed as certain as the sun rising in the eastern sky.

Bart asked, “If you couldn’t sail for Italy, which country would you sail for?”

Chris did not hesitate. “I would sail for any country...any country that would sail all the way to China.”

“You can’t get to China on the oceans. You must go by land, Chris.” Bart said it wearily, as if they had argued about it a hundred times before.

“God help me!” Chris flushed pink. “Every boy in Italy knows Marco Polo went east by land to reach China, and every boy knows no one can go that way any more. The Turks stop any Christian traveler. A new way must be found.” Chris pulled two thick ropes, each as long as his arms, from a bag. He knew Bart was gawking at the ropes but before Bart could ask what he was going to do with the ropes, Chris

"I WOULD SAIL FOR ANY COUNTRY"

continued, “The Portuguese will find a way to sail to China on the oceans.”

“The Portuguese!” Bart snickered. His eyes left the ropes. “You think the Portuguese are the best sailors in the world.”

Screeches of soaring sea gulls were like music to Chris. The salty breeze off the Mediterranean Sea was like the finest spice. He calmed down as he tied knots with the ropes. “The king of Portugal sends all his ships south along the coast of Africa. He believes that somewhere to the south the great hot land of Africa must end. Then, the ships will be able to turn and sail east to China.”

“But his ships have never found the end of Africa,” objected Bart. “They’ve been trying for many, many years.”

“I know. But there may be another way...”

“Oh no. Not that crazy idea again!”

“It isn’t crazy if the world is round like a ball, like

"NOT THAT CRAZY IDEA AGAIN!"

the ancient wizard Aristotle said. If the world is round like a ball, why couldn't a Portuguese ship sail west across the Atlantic Ocean and get to China?"

"Because it's too far! Even the Portuguese aren't that adventurous, Chris."

"Then I will have to cross the Atlantic Ocean myself."

Bart didn't snicker. Chris sounded too determined. Bart joked softly, "You are crazy enough to try it, Chris. But Father will make you a weaver instead."

Chris glanced up the terraced hillside toward his father's house and shop. He groaned. "I can't sit still all day and weave wool into cloth like Father does—and his father did before him."

"Our grandfather started working as an apprentice with a weaver at twelve. Father started working with a weaver at eleven. You are fourteen, Chris."

"Father won't apprentice me to a weaver. He

"THEN I WILL HAVE TO CROSS THE ATLANTIC OCEAN MYSELF"

needs me too much to handle his little wine and cheese business to apprentice me."

"But, that little business may fail, Chris."

Chris didn't want to face that truth. The Columbus Wine and Cheese Shop was barely making a profit. His father was a skilled weaver but never satisfied with just one business. He tried to add one small business after another and each one sputtered, then failed.

Finally, Chris replied, "I can't disobey Father. The Heavenly Father says so. But I can't be a weaver either."

"What can you do about it?"

In his darkest moments Chris had thought about running away. In Genoa, many boys his age ran away. But Chris knew from what he had learned in church that running away was wrong. He knew how deeply it would hurt his mother, Susanna, too. But he could not be a weaver. He had to convince his

RUNNING AWAY WAS WRONG

father Dominic that he loved the sea so much that making him a weaver would be like locking a powerful eagle inside a cage. But did he know enough about the sea to know if he really loved the sea?

Finally he answered Bart, "I must know what sailing the sea is really like. I don't mean just sailing a short way out into the sea to anchor all night and net sardines. I've already done that..."

"You've done that already?" cried Bart.

"The boat left after dark. I was back on shore before daybreak. Do you remember the morning you and Father were so surprised to see me already dressed and eating breakfast in the kitchen?"

"So that was why!"

"The trip was wonderful, but it wasn't enough to let me know if I really love the sea. I want to sail way out into the sea. I want to look at salt water stretching to the horizon in every direction. I want to discover a blue dot on the horizon. I want to

"I MUST KNOW WHAT SAILING THE SEA IS REALLY LIKE"

watch that dot grow bigger and bigger like it's growing out of the sea and turn as green as the most perfect emerald..."

"Land ahoy!" Bart jumped into the air.

"Yes. Some strange, beautiful new land," gushed Chris. His eyes were dreamy.

"How will you ever do that?"

"There is a real sailing ship leaving tomorrow morning for Corsica."

"The French island of Corsica? That's one hundred miles away!"

"The ship is going after a great catch of fish. The captain said I looked big enough to help pull in the nets. He said I looked big enough to snag fish caught in the nets and throw them into a huge storage area of the ship called a 'hold'. I didn't tell him how old I am and he didn't ask."

Bart smiled. "So that's why you are practicing knots."

"YES...SOME STRANGE, BEAUTIFUL NEW LAND"

"How could anyone be a sailor and not know how to tie knots?" At that moment, Chris put the final tug on a knot.

A voice behind them growled, "That's a nice bowline knot."

A second voice rumbled, "Are you coming to sea with us, boys? The pay is short, and the hours are long."

The two sailors laughed and walked on down toward the docks. Red wool stocking caps covered their heads. Gold rings glittered from their ears. Their dark arms and faces carried vivid white scars. Their hands had big knuckles and crooked fingers. Long knives were tucked inside their belts.

Bart's face became pale. "Are you going to sail with men like that tomorrow?"

Chris took a deep breath. "Yes. I'm going to sail tomorrow morning, and you're going to have to tell Father I'll be gone for a while. Now, we have to get

"THE PAY IS SHORT AND THE HOURS ARE LONG"

back to work."

Chris walked away without saying anything more.

"Christopher Columbus, are you joking?" snapped Bart in a stern voice exactly as his father Dominic would ask it. But Bart knew Chris was not joking. Tomorrow, Chris really was going to sail with dark, dangerous men out into the vast unknown sea...

BART KNEW CHRIS WAS NOT JOKING

"HOW OLD IS IT?"

CHAPTER 2

On his way up the hillside, Chris trudged past the church called Saint Mary's. Men were standing above him on wooden scaffolds repairing the outside of the church. Chris stopped to listen to the men talk. He always did that. He was too poor to go to school, but he found that by listening to older people he could learn much. How else could he have learned so much about making maps and sailing and a hundred other things he had never actually done himself?

One man on the scaffold grumbled, "This church has been here since Noah!"

"Not quite," laughed another man.

Chris couldn't keep from shouting up, "How old is it?"

The laughing man looked down at Chris. "No one remembers for sure."

Chris was amazed. “How can that be?”

The man said, “It’s been here almost since our Savior died and rose again.”

Chris muttered, “This is the year 1465.” He was stunned. He shouted, “Do you mean this building is over 1400 years old?”

The man was very serious now. “Like I said: no one knows for sure. But it’s more than a thousand years old.”

One thousand years! Chris thought about that as he walked up the narrow street. Within seconds he spotted another church, the one called Saint Don’s. His mother, Susanna, said it was over three hundred years old. Seconds later, Chris passed Saint Augustine’s. His sister, Bianchetta, had told him that church was two hundred years old.

He stopped and scanned the terraced city of Genoa. Some new churches were being built at that very moment. Steeples of old and new churches

"IT'S MORE THAN A THOUSAND YEARS OLD"

climbed into the sky all over Genoa. Today for the first time, he realized that churches had been in Genoa for over a thousand years. And so churches would be in Genoa a thousand years from now. This reality seemed to have a special meaning for him alone. It reminded him that God was the central fact of his world. And it seemed to be telling him he was about to do something that would disappoint God.

"God help me! How could I put such a burden on Bart?" he scolded himself. He marched straight into his father's weaving shop. He said gruffly, "Father, I want to go away for a few days on a fishing ship."

"What!" His father Dominic leaped away from his loom. His face was as hard as a rock. "Is the sea in your blood?"

"I think so."

"And if I say no?"

"Then it is God's will."

His father's face softened. "Who is the captain?"

"IS THE SEA IN YOUR BLOOD?"

"Mario Bono."

"Bono? The sailors say he is a good captain."

"Yes, they do."

"How could a boy of Genoa not think he loves the sea? Go and find out for yourself, Chris. I did."

"You did?"

"Yes. I was sick the entire voyage." His father smiled but almost turned green remembering it.

The next morning, Chris sat at the rear of the sailing ship and watched Genoa grow smaller. First, the red-tiled roofs of Genoa sank below the horizon and finally, the green hills beyond Genoa turned blue and melted into the horizon. Now the sea stretched in every direction, a vast blanket of shimmering blues and greens.

Captain Bono sat nearby gripping the horizontal handle called a tiller. The tiller controlled the rudder, which could change the direction of the ship.

Chris was wondering how the captain knew where

CHRIS SAT AT THE REAR OF THE SAILING SHIP

they were. Chris knew an instrument called a quadrant was used to determine a ship's distance north or south from the equator. But a quadrant could only be used at night by sighting it on a star. So how did the captain know where they were? Or how did he know how to get where they were going? The captain seemed so stern; for once Chris was afraid to ask questions. He prayed silently for courage.

"Homesick, boy?" asked the captain.

"No, sir." Chris smiled. Captain Bono's remark was the encouragement Chris needed. He quickly asked, "Where are your maps, sir?"

"I don't need any maps to find Corsica!"

The sea in every direction was now bewildering to Chris. The waves were higher now, too. He asked nervously, "How do you navigate? How do you know where we are? How do you know where we are going?"

"HOW DO YOU KNOW WHERE WE ARE?"

"Come over here. See that box? Lift that lid."

Chris lifted the lid on a small wooden box. Inside was a bowl with a circular paper divided into thirty-two parts. In the center of the paper was a short wooden peg. Balanced on the peg was an iron needle pointed on one end. The needle was free to move and quivered with every movement of the ship.

Chris said, "It's a compass."

"That's right. What direction is the sharp end of the needle pointing?"

"North." Chris knew the sharp end of the needle was magnetized, so it always pointed to the magnetic pole of the earth. And the magnetic pole was north. Every boy and girl who lived in a seaport knew that. Captain Bono had the ship headed the same direction as the blunt end of the needle. So Chris said, "We are headed south. But where is Corsica?"

"WE ARE HEADED SOUTH"

"Straight south of Genoa."

"So we can't miss Corsica...as long as we keep sailing straight south."

"Yes. I am navigating by a method known a 'dead reckoning.'"

"And the wind is at our backs."

"We call that kind of sailing 'scudding.'"

"Sailing is easy."

"*Scudding* is easy." The captain smiled as if he was amused about something. "Scudding is very fast, too. We will reach Corsica before the sun goes down."

Chris watched the southern horizon the entire day. He wanted to be the first sailor to spot land—even though none of the other sailors seemed to care. And none of the other sailors seemed to wan to talk to him.

In the late afternoon Chris spotted a tiny dark

"WE WILL REACH CORSICA BEFORE THE SUN GOES DOWN"

speck on the horizon. As soon as he was absolutely sure it was growing up out of the sea he was going to shout as loud as he could shout: "Land ahoy!"

Suddenly the captain yelled, "All hands, fasten down the sails. We are going to drop anchors."

Chris pointed to the dark speck on the horizon. "Corsica is still far off."

The captain scowled. "It's very dangerous to anchor a ship close to land with the wind blowing in toward the land. Now get busy on those sails."

Even as Chris helped with the sails he asked the captain, "How do you know there is good fishing here?"

"I've been here many times. We are close to a knob that rises off the sea bottom. The knob always has good fishing. Besides, don't you see small fish jumping up out of the water here? That can be a sign that they are being chased by a school of mackerel."

"HOW DO YOU KNOW THERE IS GOOD FISHING HERE?"

Chris helped pull thick hemp ropes that rolled th
sails around long horizontal wooden beams. Soon
the ship drifted easily with only three tall thick mast
towering into the sky.

By nightfall, they had dropped a heavy anchor of
each end of the ship. The ship bobbed on low waves
Chris helped men unload the huge net into the sea of
one side of the ship. The net was a complicated mas
of rope and hemp webbing and lead weights an
cork bobbers.

The men placed oil lamps all around the railing o
the ship. One man cooed, "Come to my bright light
my pretty little moths." But Chris knew the man wa
cooing to fish, not moths.

Men rowed away from the ship in two smal
boats. They were dragging one edge of the big ne
away from the ship.

Captain Bono yelled, "Drop the nets!" Chri

THE SHIP BOBBED ON LOW WAVES

knew the men in the small boats released the edge o
the net with lead weights. He knew the net woul
sink deep into the water with one edge still floatin
because it was held afloat by cork bobbers.

It was a long time before the captain yelled, "Al
hands, haul in the net!"

The men on board pulled on thick ropes. I
seemed like hours before they could get the ne
hauled close to the ship. And then the edge wit
cork bobbers, and the edge with lead weights had t
be pulled snug against the side of the ship by ropes
attached to the towering masts.

The net seemed alive. Chris yelled, "Thousands
of fish are squirming in the net!"

Silvery fish shimmered in the light of the lamps.
Men began to snag the fish with hooks held in their
hands and flip the fish slithering into the hold in the
center of the ship. Chris could name every kind of

THE NET SEEMED ALIVE

fish in the sea since he could remember. Everyone in Genoa ate fish every day. In the net were many long stout mackerels as heavy as small dogs. And there were thousands of smaller fish like bream and red mullets and sardines. Only a few weighty lunkers like sea perch strained his arm when he hooked them and hurled them toward the hold.

By dawn, they had emptied the great net. The hold was full of fish. The ship rode heavy in the sea. The sailors seemed neither overjoyed nor sad.

Chris thought they were exhausted like he was, but he was still suspicious. He asked a sailor, "What's wrong with everyone?"

The sailor had seemed dark and menacing the entire trip, but now he smiled. "You are a good worker. Maybe you will be a real sailor someday."

"Thanks, but you never answered my question."

"You are bold, too. So I will answer you. We are

"MAYBE YOU WILL BE A REAL SAILOR SOMEDAY"

happy we filled the hold with precious fish so fast. But we are sad we must now sail back to Genoa."

"What's wrong with going back to Genoa?"

"The ship and the sea will tell you better than I can." The sailor put his hand on Chris' shoulder. "Have courage, boy."

"WHAT'S WRONG WITH GOING BACK TO GENOA?"

SAILING AGAINST THE WIND WAS VERY HARD WORK!

CHAPTER 3

The sailor was right.

The ship and the sea soon told Chris: sailing against the wind was very hard work!

The ship could sail only at an angle to the wind. First, they sailed northwest. Then, they angled the ship back to sail northeast. Overall, the ship was slowly traveling straight north. This kind of sailing was called "tacking." And it was very hard work for the sailors. They had to change the position of the sails every time the ship changed directions. And all hands had been awake all night fishing.

Chris groaned to the rising sun, "Now I know why Captain Bono smiled when I said sailing was easy."

The captain shouted orders and the sailors repeated them. Sailing terms Chris had heard all his life became reality. Starboard, buntline, grommet, stern, staysail, block, port, halyard, clewline, bow, brace, lift, leach, furl, bowline, plus dozens of terms Chris had never heard before at all, swirled around the ship. He had so many things he must learn about a ship and sailing!

The sailors worked all day and all through the night again. They began to take turns taking naps. Chris found that he could stretch out in the smallest, hardest, smelliest, noisiest, space imaginable and go to sleep in seconds.

Genoa never looked more inviting than it did the next morning. And yet, the sailors were not done with their work. They had to unload thousands of fish onto the pier. That task would take most of the day. Chris and some other sailors had to hang the great net on racks on shore. There they sponged the webbing with a solution from buckets.

"Why are we doing this?" asked Chris. He was never too tired to ask questions.

"WHY ARE WE DOING THIS?"

A sailor grunted, "We clean the net with lime and water. Otherwise, our precious net would rot."

Chris lost all track of time. He couldn't remember if he had been gone from home two whole days or three whole days. He scarcely remembered Captain Bono walking him home after dark and giving him some silver coins. He barely remembered his mother tucking him in bed while Bart peppered him with questions he was too tired to answer.

The first thing Chris heard the next morning when he woke up was his sister Bianchetta. She cried, "Poor Chris. He's sunburned as red as his hair. His clothes are rags. He looks terrible. How he must have hated it!"

But it didn't take Chris one heartbeat to blurt, "Sailing the sea is the most wonderful thing on this earth I could ever imagine. Surely, God intends me to be a sailor!"

His father Dominic was by the bed, too. "Didn't

"SURELY GOD INTENDS ME TO BE A SAILOR!"

you get seasick, Chris?"

"No." Chris was surprised. He knew some people like his father got sick on a ship no matter how hard they tried not to get sick. But during the voyage, Chris had never even once thought about getting sick.

His mother said, "Your hands are raw."

"I must make them tougher. Sailors need very tough hands." Chris now admired sailors so much he could barely speak of them without grinning like a fool. And he admired most of all a man who could lead those tough brave sailors—the captain. If only he could be a captain!

His youngest brother, Giovanni, became very pale as he stared at Chris' red, raw hands. "I don't think I want to go to sea."

Bart laughed. "Good. Father needs one son to be a weaver. I'm going to sea with Chris."

Mother gave Chris and Bart red stocking caps

"I'M GOING TO SEA WITH CHRIS"

like all the sailors wore. She said, "It is God's will, Dominic. The love of the sea is His gift to these two boys."

From that moment, the Columbus family knew Chris and Bart were meant for the sea. Dominic let the two brothers have every opportunity to sail along the coast to deliver cheese or woolen goods. The boys became superb sailors of the small sailboats they rented. No one in the Columbus family doubted the two would leave the first time they were old enough to join the crew of a real sea-going ship.

That time came first for Chris. He was twenty when he became a sailor on a ship from Genoa that sailed all the way to the north coast of Africa. Chris learned then and there that a sailor had to do anything that his captain commanded. His captain wanted to recapture a ship that had been captured by notorious pirates called Corsairs, so the crew had to fight the pirates to recapture the ship. Chris didn't

THAT TIME CAME FIRST FOR CHRIS

like fighting but the sea was often a lawless place, and he knew God intended him to sail the sea.

From other sailors he learned by heart the verses in Psalm 107 that explained why sailors from the most ancient times put their trust in God:

"Others went out to the sea in ships;
they were merchants on the mighty waters.
They saw the works of the Lord,
his wonderful deeds in the deep.
For he spoke and stirred up a tempest
that lifted high the waves.
They mounted up to the heavens and went
down to the depths;
in their peril their courage melted away.
They reeled and staggered like drunken men:
they were at their wits' end.
Then they cried out to their Lord in their
trouble,

THE SEA WAS OFTEN A LAWLESS PLACE

and he brought them out of their distress.
He stilled the storm to a whisper;
the waves of the sea were hushed.
They were glad when it grew calm,
and he guided them to their desired haven.
Let them give thanks to the Lord for his unfailing love
and his wonderful deeds for men."

For several years Chris sailed back and forth on ships all the way to the coast of Turkey where men from Genoa held the island of Chios. On the island grew trees that yielded a precious resin called mastic, which was used in varnishes and paints. Ships loaded mastic, then sailed around the Mediterranean Sea selling it at seaports.

By now, Chris had learned all about sailing. He not only knew how to sail a ship of any size, but he knew in his heart he could command a ship. He had

HE KNEW IN HIS HEART HE COULD COMMAND A SHIP

watched the captains. He was sure he could do as well. In the back of his mind he never forgot his boyhood dream of finding a sea route to China. If only he were the captain of his own ship...

On one voyage, Chris sailed aboard the ship *Bechalla* in a fleet of five ships. This voyage was very special. After the ships loaded mastic at Chios, they sailed completely out of the Mediterranean Sea into the vast Atlantic Ocean—the ocean that had no known limits!

The fleet planned to sail north and sell the precious mastic in Portugal, Holland, and England. On August 13, 1476, the five ships left the Mediterranean and were sailing north off the coast of Portugal. Chris was high above the *Bechalla* in the crow's nest, a box at the top of the mast. He was the lookout for the ship. He was very good by now at guessing distances at sea. He knew the *Bechalla* was about six miles from the golden sands of the

HE WAS THE LOOKOUT FOR THE SHIP

Portuguese shoreline.

Suddenly, he spotted white dots on the northern horizon of the ocean. Could the dots be sails of other ships?

He strained his eye through the telescope. Then, he shouted to his captain below, "Ships ahoy! Dead ahead!"

The captain yelled up, "Friend or foe?"

Chris' eye never left the ships. He soon yelled, "They fly the flags of France!"

"How many?" hollered his captain.

Now Chris didn't want to believe his eyes as he counted. He shouted down, "Thirteen!"

He heard a worried voice below gasp, "Surely, they know we are friendly merchants..."

Water burst in the air near the *Bechalla*. A dreaded booming sound reached their ears. Soon, water was spouting in the air all around their five ships. The air was full of booms. They were being

"SHIPS AHOY! DEAD AHEAD!"

fired upon by cannons!

Wood cracked and splintered as one cannon ball crashed into the *Bechalla*. Soon their own five ships were firing cannons at the attacking ships.

"God help me!" blurted Chris. "We are going to have a great sea battle."

One enemy ship headed straight at the *Bechalla*. Neither it nor the *Bechalla* carried heavy cannons. Chris knew immediately what would happen next. The ships would ram each other. Men would scramble about, fighting knife to knife, sword to sword, hand to hand. Chris scurried down the mast. He could not help his ship in the crow's nest.

He landed on deck and raced to the rail facing the enemy ship. Members of his crew were grabbing weapons. Chris found a sword.

The enemy ship was so close, he could see the faces of its crew. The sight of them made him sick. They were sailors like himself. There was no anger

THEY WERE SAILORS LIKE HIMSELF

in their faces—only fear. Why should men do this t each other?

One sailor jumped from the enemy ship into th rigging of the *Bechalla*. In a flash, he dropped to th deck beside Chris. Chris raised his sword bu hesitated. He watched numbly as the sailor's swor slashed into his own shoulder. Chris swung hi sword wildly at the sailor and backed him away.

A voice screamed, "Fire!"

Chris smelled smoke. The *Bechalla* was on fire

The enemy ship was flaming too!

The sailor who had struck Chris dropped hi sword. He had no stomach for fighting now. It wa obvious now there would be no cargo to steal There wouldn't even be a ship left. Both ships wer going to burn up and sink!

Men on both ships stopped fighting and began throwing wooden barrels and boards into the ocean—anything that could float. Maybe some sailors coul

THE BECHALLA WAS ON FIRE!

survive if they were lucky enough to grab something that floated. And, if they floated toward shore and not farther out into the Atlantic.

But what if the captain of the *Bechalla* wanted to fight to the bitter end? Chris would have to stay, too. He looked up to see the great sails in flames. His captain screamed, "All hands! Abandon ship!"

Chris stood at the rail facing Portugal. Six miles of choppy ocean separated him from its friendly shore. Chris was not a good swimmer. He had heard many stories about savage bloodthirsty sharks too. And now blood streamed from his shoulder down his arm...

"Please, God," he prayed. "Help me. In the name of Jesus."

And he leaped into the black ocean...

" PLEASE, GOD... HELP ME. IN THE NAME OF JESUS "

GOD HAD ANSWERED HIS PLEA

CHAPTER 4

Chris was swallowed by the sea. He gagged on salt water. He fought for air. He flailed his arms and kicked his feet against the heavy sea. The sea yanked him under. Was this his destiny? Was a watery grave God's plan for him? He prayed for God's help.

His hand hit something. For a heartbeat, he worried it was a shark. But no. It felt flat and rough. It was rough wood. From the ship. He lunged at it and hugged the plank of coarse wood. God had answered his plea.

"Thank you, God!" yelled Chris. "Now I must find the shore."

He searched the sky. He had the sailor's habit of knowing what the weather was doing every moment. Just before the battle, he watched the cloud puffs streaming in toward the land. Now, he would kick his feet and follow those same clouds!

It was hours before he heard the roar. What was it? Would he never reach safety after all? His foot struck bottom. Could the roar be the sound of waves breaking on the shore? The waves got bigger. He felt himself thrust forward. He and his plank rolled onto a beach.

Many people were scrambling over the sands of the beach. Chris understood enough Portuguese to learn that they were from a nearby village. They had heard the booms of cannons. They had watched the battle. Now they were helping the lucky sailors who struggled onto the beach and coughed water from their lungs.

"I am Italian," Chris tried to explain in Portuguese.

The people didn't care which ship Chris sailed on. One woman cleaned his wound and wrapped it with cloth. Her husband helped Chris walk to their hut in

"I AM ITALIAN"

the village. While Chris rested there, he realized what a terrible mess he was in. He was stranded in a foreign country. He owned nothing but the clothes on his back. The money he had saved and his extra clothing were at the bottom of the sea!

"But thank God for my most precious possession of life," Chris told himself. "I'm always in God's hands. Somehow, this great mess will turn into something better for me." Hadn't he always trusted God?

A few days later, Chris joined a long line of barefoot sailors walking to Lisbon, the capital of Portugal. They all had to find work again as soon as possible. They had lost everything too. Chris became excited as he walked. The Portuguese were the best sailors in the world. And Lisbon was the most important seaport in the world.

After he walked into the lively city, he discovered that many people from Genoa lived there. He

THEY HAD TO FIND WORK AGAIN AS SOON AS POSSIBLE

quickly found work with a man from Genoa who made maps of the sea. There were so many sea captains in Lisbon, the man couldn't make maps of the sea fast enough to supply them all.

Helping make maps was a wonderful job for Chris, who loved to look at maps. But Chris warned the mapmaker, "I am a sailor. I can work on maps only between voyages."

"I don't mind," answered the mapmaker. "You are such a good helper, you may work for me between voyages."

Chris got a wonderful idea. "I'll write brother Bart to ask him to come to Lisbon. The two of us can make maps for you when we're not at sea."

The mapmaker said, "Thank you. Ten men can't make the maps fast enough to supply all the sea captains."

Chris regularly attended a church nearby. The church was associated with a boarding school for

HELPING MAKE MAPS WAS A WONDERFUL JOB

girls from well-to-do families. The girls were educated and very polite. Chris was not confident enough to speak to them. But at night, he began to educate himself furiously in mathematics and reading Latin and Portuguese. He carefully observed how such educated well-to-do people behaved, so he would have good manners, too. He was sure even a simple weaver's son could do anything with God's help.

After Bart arrived, Chris left on a voyage to Iceland. Iceland was an island nearly 2000 miles north of Lisbon. Chris realized he had now sailed as far north on the Atlantic Ocean as any men had ever sailed. He learned how sailors could carry enough supplies to stay at sea for very long periods of time. And he also noted shrewdly that when ships sailed toward the north, the winds from the west became very strong, so that it was very difficult to sail straight west.

CHRIS LEFT ON A VOYAGE TO ICELAND

Chris was getting a reputation for being very smart at sea. Soon after his voyage to Iceland, a man from Genoa gave Chris the opportunity he had prayed for since he was fourteen. The man let Chris captain his ship! Chris sailed the ship west to the Azores, the farthest known islands of the western Atlantic. There he picked up sugar and delivered it to a seaport in the Mediterranean Sea.

While sailing to the Azores, Chris had stopped at the island of Porto Santo. He little realized how that short stop would change his life. But a few weeks after successfully completing his first voyage as captain, following the church service at the chapel in Lisbon, he overheard one of the older girls say, "My brother is the Governor of Porto Santo."

His knees were shaky. His mouth was dry. But Chris prayed for God's help and seized the opportunity. He said politely, "Excuse me, but I sail occasionally to Porto Santo. Perhaps I could deliver a

"EXCUSE ME, BUT I SAIL OCCASIONALLY TO PORTO SANTO"

message to your brother. I am Christopher Columbus."

The girl hesitated. Should she talk to this tall, red-haired stranger? Chris acted very serious. Finally, she smiled. "I am Felipa Pestrello. How do you like our little island in the great sea?"

"Porto Santo is a lovely island."

After that moment, neither one groped for reasons to speak. Words and tender looks flowed freely. Both were shy, yet not shy with each other. And before the hour was over, Chris knew that he had met the third great love of his life. God was first. Before he had met Felipa, the sea had been second. But now when he looked into her eyes, he loved her more than the sea.

Chris met Felipa's mother. Felipa's father, who had also been Governor of Porto Santo as well as a sea captain, was dead. Chris learned that the father of Felipa's mother was Gill Moniz, a sea captain

HE LOVED HER MORE THAN THE SEA

who had sailed for Prince Henry of Portugal. The Pestrellos actually knew the royal family of Portugal! How could they ever accept Chris, the son of a simple wool weaver?

Chris courted Felipa a long time anyway and asked her to marry him. He wasn't surprised when she accepted his proposal. But what about her family? Why would they accept him? But they did accept him. Chris was a sea captain—a sea captain just like the men who had built the reputation of their family.

He and Felipa settled in Porto Santo, far out west in the Atlantic Ocean. They lived with her mother and her brother, the Governor of the island. And in 1480, they were blessed with a baby boy and named him Diego. Chris still sailed often. He sailed 1500 miles south down the African coast, then 1500 miles east into the Gulf of Guinea—as far south as any man had ever sailed.

THEY WERE BLESSED WITH A BABY BOY

He heard a man in Italy named Toscanelli who believed that China was only 5000 miles west of Portugal and Spain. Chris wrote him a letter and asked him to explain why he thought that was true. Toscanelli sent back a letter and answered him with what Chris considered very convincing arguments.

Yet, Chris began to wonder if he had already abandoned his lifelong dream of sailing west to find a sea route to China. He had never even told Felipa about it. He prayed to God for an answer.

One day he walked the beach of Porto Santo with Felipa and Diego, who was now old enough to examine every sea shell and try to mold every sand grain into a castle. The beach was peppered with Diego's old sand castles.

Felipa laughed into the soft sea breeze. "You always walk with Diego to this beach that faces west, Chris."

"I do?"

"YOU ALWAYS WALK TO THIS BEACH THAT FACES WEST"

"Yes. And while Diego plays here, you wait as if there is something you are looking for." Felipa bent over Diego and took his hand. "What is Diego playing with?"

Chris looked at the small round pod in Diego's chubby hand. "It's called a sea bean. It's really a seed pod from a tree."

"Which tree?" shouted Diego. He looked around eagerly.

Chris laughed. "No one I know has ever seen the tree they come from."

"I played with those pods as a child too," said Felipa, smiling as Diego skipped away to begin a sand castle. "They are found only on this beach on the west side of the island. Where do they come from?"

"They float on the sea and come up on the beach, especially after great storms from the west. So somewhere in the far, far west, they fall from a tree

" I PLAYED WITH THOSE PODS AS A CHILD TOO "

perhaps no European but Marco Polo has ever seen. The tree grows perhaps on land no European but Marco Polo has ever seen."

"China! Could someone sail west to get there?"

"It would be a very long voyage. It would take a captain with a great knowledge of the sea."

"My brother brags to everyone that you may be the only sea captain who has sailed to every limit of the Atlantic— north, south, and west."

Chris was stunned. Were important people saying such things about him? "It would take more than a good captain. It would take several ships, many good sailors, and many supplies. I could not afford it."

"The king of Portugal can afford it." Felipa sounded very excited.

"Portugal only tries to sail to the south around Africa. They are still trying. Portugal is not interested in a western sea route to China."

"I COULD NOT AFFORD IT"

"But, Chris, we have a new king—King John."

"I didn't know the old king. I don't know the new king. A king won't see just anybody."

"My brother knows him."

"But why would your brother stake his reputation on my dreams of a sea route to China?"

"So you have always wanted to do it! My brother will help you. I just know he will."

And she rushed Chris and Diego to her brother, the Governor.

"MY BROTHER WILL HELP YOU"

"YOUR EXCELLENCY..."

CHAPTER 5

"Of course, I'll help!" exclaimed her brother.

He wrote a letter to the king that explained who Chris was. Later Chris sailed with Felipa and Diego to Lisbon, so Chris could present his plan to the new king of Portugal—King John! In Lisbon, Bart gave him a pep talk before the meeting. Felipa kept encouraging him, too. After all, hadn't Saint Paul and even the Savior himself embarked on much greater missions by the age of thirty? And, Chris was now over thirty years old.

Minutes later, Chris could scarcely believe he was actually kneeling before the king of Portugal. On his knees,Chris prayed silently for God's will to be done. But he couldn't help hoping that his plan was God's plan, too.

Chris stood up, tall and square-shouldered. He started in a soft, polite voice, "Your Excellency, I wish to propose a plan which will bring great fame to Portugal."

King John laughed. "Do you think Portugal needs more fame?"

Chris felt his face flush. He calmly pushed on. "Portugal has always looked for a sea route to China."

"And we will find it. Captain Dias thinks he can sail to the southern tip Of Africa,and then sail east to China..."

"I have a plan to find a different sea route," said Chris with great patience.

"Why should I listen to you at all?" But King John said it mischievously—like he already knew about Chris and his plan.

"Your Excellency, I've sailed Portuguese ships with Portuguese crews to the northern, southern, and western limits of the Atlantic Ocean," boasted Chris in a loud voice.

"WHY SHOULD I LISTEN TO YOU AT ALL?"

And Chris began showing maps as he explained how Toscanelli calculated the distance from Portugal west to China and then told the king how many heathens were in China who could be converted to Christianity.

King John thought hard. “Do you agree that China has fabulous riches of jewels and gold?”

“Yes. but...”

“So you ask me for three ships and ninety men?”

“And a year’s supply of food,” added Chris.

“I will think it over.”

Chris waited at Bart’s house for the king’s answer.

A few days later,the answer came by royal messenger. Chris broke open the letter which was rolled shut and held tight with wax. The wax was stamped with the king’s own special seal.

The answer in the letter was a polite “no”.

Bart and Felipa debated why King John had

THE ANSWER IN THE LETTER WAS A POLITE 'NO'

turned Chris down. Had Chris asked for too much? Did the king believe China could not be reached by sailing west? Did the king think it was easier to sail around Africa?

The debate stopped when Felipa got a fever. In those days, any sickness with fever was a reason for real worry. The "Black Death," which had claimed half the lives in Europe 200 years earlier, was still feared and talked about. It was soon clear that Felipa did not have the "Black Death"—but that was no consolation to Chris. Felipa had another kind of fever that was just as deadly.

Her dying words were, "Take care of Diego—but never give up your dreams."

"Help us, God," sobbed Chris.

Chris turned to God for comfort. Not only was his lifelong dream dead; but his lifelong love was dead. It seemed life could not be worse. But he soon remembered his wife's dying words. He must take

"NEVER GIVE UP YOUR DREAMS"

care of Diego. He must realize his dream of sailing west across the Atlantic Ocean, too. She would be very disappointed in him if he didn't do those things.

But Portugal was not the answer. He said good-bye to Bart and took five-year-old Diego on a ship to Spain. The ship sailed only one hundred miles south, then one hundred miles east to dock at the port of Palos. Diego would live in a monastery at La Rabida near Palos and begin his schooling. Chris traveled on to Cordoba and tried to meet the king and queen of Spain who lived in a palace in Cordoba sometimes and in a palace in Madrid at other times.

While he waited, Chris heard many stories about the king and queen. King Ferdinand was a sly man who prided himself on outwitting other kings and queens of Europe. He would go to war, too, to win an argument. Queen Isabella was different. She tried to be very good at all times. But she was also very shrewd.

DIEGO WOULD LIVE IN A MONASTERY

Meeting with any king and queen in any country was not easy.

Many months later in 1486, Chris finally was allowed to meet them. He was shocked by the sight of Isabella. She could have been his sister. She was the same age. She had blue eyes, milky skin that flushed pink in an instant. She had reddish brown hair. He knew she was surprised at his appearance, too. They were intrigued by each other. Were they destined to share some great enterprise?

Once again, Chris argued his case for finding a western sea route to China. He was forceful, even boastful. The king and queen were impressed with Chris. But the time for his appeal was wrong. King Ferdinand was at war with the kingdom of Granada. That war required all of Spain's energy and resources, so the king and queen said no.

Chris put off sailing again. He lived in Spain and devoted himself to his plan. Bart helped him from

HE WAS SHOCKED BY THE SIGHT OF ISABELLA

Lisbon. Between the two of them, they constantly sent appeals to kings and queens all over Europe. Even King Henry VII of England and King Charles VIII of France said they might be willing to meet with Chris. Then Chris heard very bad news.

"God help me!" he cried.

King John of Portugal had encouraged two sea captains named Dulma and Estreito to attempt the western sea route proposed by Chris himself. But the captains started the voyage too far north and had to sail against strong winds called the westerlies. The westerlies battered their sails to ribbons. The captains failed. Chris became very discouraged. "Kings and queens will think my plan has been tried and was a failure."

But to his surprise, King John was not discouraged at all, but in fact, even more determined. He let Chris know he was interested in how Chris would make a similar attempt succeed. By 1488, Chris was

CHRIS BECAME VERY DISCOURAGED

back in Lisbon to present his plan again.

Bart was enthusiastic. "King John realizes now that you're the only sea captain who can carry out such a voyage."

"With God's help..." added Chris cautiously.

"Your reputation grows and grows. Now sailors are saying you are such a master of the sea, you can predict a storm days ahead of time."

Chris didn't deny that story. It was true. "It is a gift from the Heavenly Father. I don't know myself how I know a storm is coming. But I know."

"And now King John knows!"

But as Chris went into the street the next morning, people were yelling and streaming toward the docks. A man cried, "Captain Dias is back from Africa!" Soon, everyone in Lisbon knew Captain Dias had returned from his long voyage south along Africa. He claimed to have found the southern tip of Africa! Everyone knew the next step was for King

"IT IS A GIFT FROM THE HEAVENLY FATHER"

John to have a fleet of ships sail around Africa and sail east to China. And Chris knew King John was no longer interested in giving ships and supplies to a western voyage.

This discovery made for a very trying time for Chris. For three years since Felipa died, he had doggedly pursued his dream. He could find interest in his plan but no real support. Now it seemed as if there might be another sea route to China. Who would be interested in a western route now?

He felt very lonely in Spain. Felipa was dead. Diego was in school. Bart lived and worked in Lisbon. The rest of his family lived in Genoa. And Chris was not even sailing, which he was sure he did better than anyone else in the world.

"How can my life get any worse?" he complained.

He soon found out. He became the butt of jokes.

Men who had envied his influence with kings and queens now sensed he had lost all his influence with

"HOW CAN MY LIFE GET ANY WORSE?"

royalty. They openly teased Chris of being a crackpot, a man who wouldn't give up his plan that everyone but him knew was crazy. Chris relied on the Word of God for strength. He read his Bible every day.

"Consider it pure joy, my brothers," he read in the first chapter of James, "whenever you face trials of many kinds, because you know that the testing of your faith develops perseverance. Perseverance must finish its work so that you may be mature and complete..." Chris believed James with all his heart. God must think he was not quite mature enough yet.

His Bible convinced him not to brood over the stinging jokes or over his bad luck. He used the time to educate himself more. The printing press, invented thirty years before in Germany, had been used for printing books in Spain for over ten years. Books, once printed by hand and expensive, were now abundant and cheap. Chris borrowed many

"PERSEVERANCE MUST FINISH ITS WORK"

books. He read books on plants, animals, geography, and mathematics. And he practiced and practiced Spanish until he learned it as well as he had learned Portuguese.

Yet, when Ferdinand and Isabella agreed to see him again he was reluctant to go. Spain's war with Granada was not over. "How many times must I fail?" he asked himself.

The king and queen sent him money for a new suit of clothes and a donkey to ride to the palace. Chris was very embarrassed. They surely knew how poor he had become in the six years he had been living in Spain and not sailing the oceans. But Chris appeared in his new clothes and fearlessly presented his plan once again. Queen Isabella's eyes were sympathetic. Even King Ferdinand paid attention. But Ferdinand was a playful scheming man. Was he tricking Chris only to keep him from seeing Ferdinand's rivals, the kings of France and England?

CHRIS FEARLESSLY PRESENTED HIS PLAN ONCE AGAIN

Ferdinand and Isabella sent him away without an answer. Life among powerful people was so trying.

Weeks later, Spain's war with Granada ended. Would the king and queen now approve his plan?

Then Chris got a royal letter! He ripped through the wax seal with trembling fingers...

CHRIS GOT A ROYAL LETTER!

"GOD HELP ME... SIX YEARS I'VE WAITED!"

CHAPTER 6

The royal letter was only the answer from the king and queen to his last appeal. The answer was "no."

"God help me!" he cried. "Six years I've waited. I'm leaving for France!"

He loaded his few belongings on the donkey. He would ride north to France. It was a very long, rough trip to Paris. But he couldn't afford to travel to Paris on a ship. Somehow the donkey would get him there. Hadn't the Savior ridden a donkey?

Within a few miles on his humble way out of Spain, he was stopped by a royal messenger.

The messenger snapped, "You are to see the king and queen right away!" And he escorted Chris to the royal court.

In the royal court, Chris watched as a man named Luis Santangel asked to speak for a group of men to the king and queen. *Oh no*, thought Chris, *once again advisers who know nothing about sailing are going to tell the king and queen why my plan won't work.* Why did they want Chris here? He already knew their answer was "no."

Santangel said calmly, "This man Christopher Columbus asks for three ships, ninety men, and a supply of food for one year..."

King Ferdinand interrupted, "Yes, he asks for much. And the risk of his plan is very great..."

Santangel smiled. "In return he offers Spain the chance to spread Christianity throughout a new empire."

The king blurted, "And all the jewels and gold and silver his ships can carry back to Spain!" The king stopped abruptly as he realized he was arguing for Chris' plan.

Santangel smiled again. "Yes, the rewards for the success of this voyage are very great indeed. That is why my group of businessmen will pay for his

"THE RISKS OF HIS PLAN ARE VERY GREAT"

voyage if he is allowed to sail under the protection of the Spanish flag."

Chris was shocked. Santangel supported his plan. And he had made it so easy for the king and queen to accept. They risked no money at all. But would they refuse anyway? Would they be afraid to have the flag of Spain flying for a voyage that might fail?

Chris first saw the answer in the eyes of Queen Isabella. Her eyes were soft with approval.

But what about the king? No one spoke as King Ferdinand frowned a long time. Finally, the king looked at the queen and smiled, as if he was at last giving in to her.

Queen Isabella's voice was music. "Christopher Columbus, you will sail west for Spain!"

Chris spent the next ten weeks gathering three ships, their crews, and supplies. This effort took place at the port of Palos, near the monastery of La Rabida where Diego lived. Diego was now twelve

"YOU WILL SAIL WEST FOR SPAIN!"

years old. One day, Chris took Diego by horseback to the dock to show him the three ships.

When Diego saw the ships he blurted, "Take me with you, Father!"

"You are too young. My page boy is fifteen years old."

"Then I'll be a common seaman."

"Look, Diego! The largest ship there is called the *Santa Maria*," Chris pointed to a ship about eighty feet from end to end and about thirty feet across. "I will sail as captain of the fleet on that ship. It will be the flagship of the fleet."

"It's chunky. It looks slow."

"Yes." Chris didn't hide his own dislike for the bulky ship, which was called a carrack. He would have preferred another smaller but faster caravel like his other two ships, the *Pinta* and the *Niña*.

"Father," cried Diego, "one of your ships is on the beach flopped over on its side!"

THE SANTA MARIA

"That's called 'heaved down.' The sailors rolled it over on its side. They are brushing the bottom with tar to seal the cracks between boards so the ship won't leak too much. When they finish that side they will turn it on its other side and tar it too. That must be done to every ship every few months."

"Do you mean water leaks into all ships?"

"Yes. But at sea, we pump the water out of the bottom of the ship every morning with the 'bilge pump.'"

"What if the pump breaks? It sounds very dangerous to sail the seas in leaky ships."

"It takes all of a man's talents and the help of God to sail the mighty seas."

"Where do you sleep?"

"I sleep in one of those two small cabins on the end of the deck. The other officers share the other cabin."

"Where do the sailors—like myself—sleep?"

"IT TAKES THE HELP OF GOD TO SAIL THE MIGHTY SEAS"

Chris laughed. "Anywhere on the deck they can stretch out or curl up. There is no special place to sleep."

"No bed?" Diego's mouth fell open. "And where is the dining hall?"

"There is none."

"But where is the kitchen?"

"The steward simply cooks on a wood fire in that open metal box you see sitting on the deck."

"Perhaps I *am* too young to sail on the oceans."

When Chris took Diego back to the monastery he gave him a red wool stocking cap. "This is the one article of clothing all real sailors wear. Someday, Diego, you will sail the oceans with me."

Chris returned to oversee his ships and supplies. Three well-to-do families who lived in the area—the Pinzons, the Niños, and the Quinteros—were recruiting men for the crews. It was the custom for the owner of a ship to serve as "master," second in

"PERHAPS I AM TOO YOUNG TO SAIL ON THE OCEANS"

command below the captain. So the master of Chris' flagship *Santa Maria* was its owner Juan de la Cosa. The flagship was to have a total crew of forty officers and seamen.

An old man approached him. It was a struggle for him to walk. He said, "Are you Christopher Columbus?"

"Who wants to know, sir?"

"You are cautious. That is good. My name is Pedro."

"What is your last name, Pedro?"

"It is better for me if I don't tell you. In 1452 I sailed where you wish to sail."

"1452! I was one year old in 1452. I never heard of anyone sailing that far west in those times."

"You haven't heard of it because we lacked the courage to go on. But I tell you we sailed west past the Azores for Prince Henry of Portugal."

"How far west?"

"ARE YOU CHRISTOPHER COLUMBUS?"

"Far enough west to reach a mysteriously calm sea as flat as glass. No wind blew there. No waves rolled there. The flat sea was choked with seaweed."

"How did you get out then?"

"It wasn't the seaweed that stopped us. It was our lack of faith in ourselves and God. We turned and slowly sailed back."

"Thanks for warning me, Pedro."

"When you sail into that sea of weeds, push on through it. You won't get stuck in the seaweed. And it must end somewhere."

Chris didn't know whether to believe Pedro or not. He had never heard of such a thing as a sea of seaweed, and he had sailed everywhere. He would test the old man. He said casually, "The captain of the *Pinta* will be Martin Pinzon. What sort of man is he?"

"He is a brash, ambitious man. Watch him. He will have twenty-four officers and seamen who may

"THANKS FOR WARNING ME, PEDRO"

turn against you."

Pedro's answer surprised Chris. That was his opinion of Martin Pinzon too. He would test the old man again. "His brother Vincent will be captain of the *Niña*."

"Vincent Pinzon will be humble and loyal to you. Count twenty-five officers and seamen who will stand beside you."

"Plus the thirty-nine officers and seamen on my own ship."

Pedro frowned. "I've probably said too much. Martin Pinzon is very powerful in these parts."

Chris watched Pedro walk off stiffly. The old man had said some very frank, even dangerous things. Why would he lie about the sea of seaweed? But could such a story be true?

Chris inspected supplies being stacked at the dock. The ships would carry many barrels of ready-made hard biscuits, salted wheat flour, and unground

"MARTIN PINZON IS VERY POWERFUL IN THESE PARTS"

wheat. Barrels of lentils, beans, rice, and chickpeas were there to be loaded, too. Wine, olive oil, and vinegar were stored in barrels as well. And sure to be popular were casks of salted fish, salted meat, honey, raisins, cheese, and almonds.

A rich man would have thought this diet for the fleet was limited. But Chris knew from his own experience his seamen would eat as well on his ships as they did on shore. And, of course, they had fishing tackle to catch whatever fish they could catch from the ocean.

By August 3, 1492, the three ships were ready to sail. Chris said good-bye to Diego. The crews pulled the gangplanks from the docks into the ships and raised the anchors. They used long oars of ash wood called sweeps to nudge the ships gently seaward. Soon, the great sails were unfurled. They billowed out from catching the wind from the north. The ships scudded rapidly south.

BY AUGUST 3, 1492, THE THREE SHIPS WERE READY TO SAIL

Chris faced his crew. "Our first stop will be the Canary Islands!"

In his cabin, Chris sat down at a table and opened a large book. All the pages were blank. With a feather quill pen and ink he intended to record everything that happened in this log book. It would be the "Journal of the Voyage." He would record all navigational data about the course being steered, all daily work, all daily happenings, all birds sighted, all unusual fish sighted, any people encountered, and on and on. In his heart, he really believed this log book would be studied through the ages. He was a man with a mission. But he was not alone. He inked the first entry into his "Journal of the Voyage": IN THE NAME OF OUR LORD JESUS CHRIST.

'IN THE NAME OF OUR LORD JESUS CHRIST'

"HOW ARE WE DOING?"

CHAPTER 7

Chris left his cabin. "How are we doing?" he asked Juan de la Cosa.

"All three ships are scudding south like race horses, sir!"

Their great sails were pushed hard by the winds from the north called "northerlies." Of course, sailing south was exactly as Chris had planned. He had to sail south before he turned to sail straight west. He remembered only too well how Dulma and Estreito had started too far north when they had sailed west. The westerlies had battered their ships back to Portugal.

Years before, on his trips along the African coast, Chris had carefully noted how his ships eventually encountered winds called the northeast trade winds. Those trade winds pushed a ship southwest. And that is exactly how Chris intended to sail across the

Atlantic Ocean: his ships would scud west with the friendly trade winds at their backs.

He returned to his cabin. Everything was under control. He had already divided the officers and seamen into two crews. One crew worked under the master, Juan de la Cosa. The other crew worked under the pilot, Perelonso Niño. The crews alternated four-hour 'watches' beginning at the hours of three, seven, and eleven. Every day the *Santa Maria* had a very rigid routine.

Outside his cabin Chris heard a young voice sing out:

"One glass is gone
and now the second glass flows;
More shall run down
if God wills it.
To God let's pray
to give us a good voyage..."

"ONE GLASS IS GONE..."

The young seaman sang about a "sand clock," a sealed glass with two bulby sections joined by a tiny neck. The sand clock was so important, yet so fragile, that Chris kept a dozen extras in his cabin. It took exactly thirty minutes for all the sand to run from the top bulb of the glass through a tiny opening in the neck into the bottom bulb of the glass. A young seaman was given the job of turning the glass the instant the top bulb was empty. He also sang out each time which glass it was.

But that wasn't all he sang. He also sang out, "Hey, you, forward! Look alive. Keep good watch!" The young seaman had to make sure a seaman at the front of the ship was awake and keeping watch in front of the ship.

The seaman at the front was supposed to yell back, "All is well!"

Later, when it was time for Mr. Niño's crew to relieve Mr. de la Cosa's crew, the young seaman

IT TOOK THIRTY MINUTES FOR THE SAND TO RUN THROUGH

sang at the top of his lungs, "On deck! On deck! Mr. Niño's seamen! On deck in good time, you of Mr. Niño's watch, for it is already time! Shake a leg!"

Chris was always amazed at how well young seamen carried out their work with the glass. The next morning, their first real morning at sea, he was pleased to hear the young voice sing:

"Blessed be the light of day
and the holy cross, we say,
and the Lord of truth
and the holy Trinity.
Blessed be the immortal soul
and the Lord who keeps it whole.
Blessed be the light of day
and He who sends the night away!"

Chris made sure his officers and seamen never forgot they were in the hands of God. He reinforced

HE WAS PLEASED TO HEAR THE YOUNG VOICE SING

the ship's gratitude for God's help when he walked out on the deck each morning and shouted, "Thanks to God for the good sailing!"

The very first thing the morning crew did was grab a hard biscuit, a chunk of cheese, and a salted sardine for breakfast. They didn't have to dress. They never undressed, except for an occasional swim on a very calm day when the ship was barely moving. They wore no shoes. They never shaved. One main duty of the first day watch was to slosh salt water over the decks and sweep them thoroughly with stiff brooms. The other main duty was to pump sea water out of the bottom of the ship.

Each time a new crew started its watch, the helmsman, the man who was steering the ship with the tiller, would call out the course he was steering. When Mr. Niño's crew relieved Mr. de la Cosa's crew, the helmsman of Mr. de la Cosa's crew yelled, "Southwest by one quarter of the south wind!"

"THANKS TO GOD FOR THE GOOD SAILING!"

Mr. de la Cosa, of the old crew, yelled, "Southwest by one quarter of the south wind!"

Mr. Niño, of the new crew, yelled, "Southwest by one quarter of the south wind!"

Mr. Niño's helmsman yelled, "Southwest by one quarter of the south wind!"

So the course of the ship was called out in a loud voice four times, and each time was heard by no fewer than two officers and two seamen. There was no excuse for ever steering the wrong course. Today's course was slightly south of southwest, and Chris did not plan on changing that course until they spotted the Canary Islands.

Scudding was easy, even in rough seas. There was very little work to do with changing the sails. The crews were happy. They had no trouble at all keeping the deck and sails of the ship very neat and clean. When they did get orders, they were orders that could be understood only by seamen. They

THE COURSE OF THE SHIP WAS CALLED OUT IN A LOUD VOICE

were in the language of the sea:

"Clear the scuppers!"

"Well the clewlines!"

"Give the spritsail a little sheet!"

"Belay them backstays!"

The one hot meal of the day was prepared at eleven o'clock. The steward stacked wood in the metal firebox and lit a fire. Usually, he fried fresh fish or salted meat in olive oil. And sometimes, he would bake flat tortillas of wheat bread in the ashes of the fire.

Fire was also used to signal the two ships that followed. In rough seas, the three ships moved far apart for safety, so the crews were not able to yell back and forth. An iron container with a blazing fire hung like a torch off the back of the *Santa Maria*. Chris could signal at night by flashing a blanket across the torch at intervals. During the day the

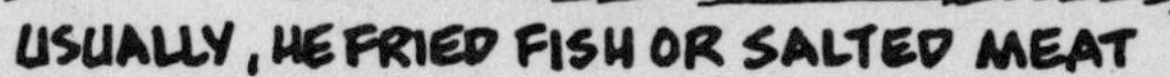

USUALLY, HE FRIED FISH OR SALTED MEAT

blanket was soaked with water so it could cause puffs of smoke to rise off the torch for a signal.

Sometimes, the other two ships had to signal the *Santa Maria.* After only three days at sea, the *Pinta* fired its cannon once—the signal for help! Chris and two seamen took the rowboat the *Santa Maria* carried and rowed to the *Pinta.* Even before Chris boarded the ship, he knew his fleet had had its first serious accident. Each ship had a huge rudder that went down into the water at the back of the ship. The helmsman steered the ship with the tiller, which turned the rudder. On the *Pinta*, the rudder was hanging loose. So the helmsman had no way to steer the ship. The *Pinta* was drifting out of control.

The captain of the *Pinta*, Martin Pinzon, confided in Chris, "I think the ship's owner Quintero tampered with the rudder!"

"But why?"

"I THINK QUINTERO TAMPERED WITH THE RUDDER"

"Because Quintero is angry that I did not make him my master, my first officer. I allowed him to come along only as an ordinary seaman."

Chris knew Quintero was angry. It was normal for the owner to be the master of his own ship. He was not master because Martin Pinzon had picked his brother Francisco Pinzon as master. But would Quintero endanger his own ship? And he was a seaman aboard the *Pinta*. Would he endanger his own life just to get even with Martin Pinzon?

Chris simply said, "I'm sure you will be able to fix the rudder. There is no way in this rough sea that the other ships can help you. We can't risk a collision. We will continue on to the Canary Islands. Meet us at the island of Las Palmas."

Back on board the *Santa Maria*, Chris thought about how a shrewd man like Martin Pinzon knew Quintero would not endanger his own life. It was

WOULD HE ENDANGER HIS OWN SHIP?

just a case where Pinzon had a problem with his ship and tried to blame someone else. That incident was not a good beginning. Chris would probably have a lot of trouble with Martin Pinzon.

Chris had wanted his own brother Bart to captain the *Pinta*—or even the *Niña*. But the Pinzon brothers would have made it very difficult to recruit crews around Palos if they were not the captains. So Bart had stayed behind. He said he did not want to make the voyage as a seaman or officer under another captain. But Chris wondered if Bart was concerned for Diego's welfare, too. Who would take care of Chris' young son Diego if Chris never returned from this dangerous voyage?

The *Santa Maria* and the *Niña* reached the island of Las Palmas in the Canary Islands with no problem. But it was almost three weeks before the *Pinta* joined them.

THE SANTA MARIA AND THE NINA REACHED LAS PALMAS

Chris was very short with Martin Pinzon. "The time has not been wasted by the men of the *Santa Maria* and *Niña*. They loaded barrel after barrel of fresh water into the holds of the two ships. They stacked piles of firewood all over the decks. They gathered fruit and nuts. They also stacked supplies on shore for the *Pinta*. See that your men load the *Pinta* right away, Mr. Pinzon."

While the men loaded supplies on the *Pinta*, Chris met a Spanish sailor who had just sailed from Ferro, the island farthest west in the Canary Islands. The sailor said he had heard three Portuguese warships were waiting at Ferro to ambush Columbus. King John did not want Spain to explore the western Atlantic.

"God, help me!" Chris exploded inside his cabin, where his men could not hear him. "My fleet is equipped to explore a new way to China, not fight

"GOD HELP ME!"

the Portuguese!"

His fleet carried no soldiers, only sailing officers and seamen. Each of his ships had a couple of small cannons and a couple of scatter-guns that were even smaller.

Yet, he had no choice. Chris prayed to God. His fleet must sail on, whether Portuguese warships waited or not...

HIS FLEET MUST SAIL ON

"OUR FLAGSHIP COULDN'T ESCAPE FROM A ROWBOAT_"

CHAPTER 8

September 6th, the first morning out at sea from Las Palmas, Chris stood at the rear of the ship in front of his cabin. His first officer Juan de la Cosa was nearby at the tiller.

After one hour of sailing, De la Cosa muttered, "Our flagship couldn't escape from a rowboat, let alone Portuguese warships!"

Chris had to agree. His flagship *Santa Maria* plowed down into the waves. The other two ships almost had to sail in circles in order to slow down enough to wait for his ship, which was plowing along no faster than one mile per hour.

"All hands!" yelled Chris. "Unlash the piles of firewood from the front of the ship and move them toward the back. Get down in the hold and move the barrels of water we added in Las Palmas toward the back of the ship!"

Those were very big jobs. The crew had spent days in Las Palmas loading the new supplies and tying them down. But all hands carried out his orders as if they were on fire. After all, they knew what a Portuguese warship could do. Inch by inch the front of the *Santa Maria* rose out of the water. And the ship moved faster and faster across the open ocean.

Chris had his fleet sail past Ferro on the north or windward side, reasoning that if the Portuguese warships were waiting they would have to be anchored on the protected side of the island because it is very dangerous to anchor on the windward side of land.

Soon his three ships sailed well beyond Ferro. Portuguese sails were nowhere in sight. The danger was over. The Portuguese warships would have to search the Atlantic Ocean for them—a hopeless task. And the fleet of Portuguese warships was not

HIS THREE SHIPS SAILED WELL PAST FERRO

equipped for a long voyage like his fleet was.

Chris heard the young seaman singing the changing of the sand clock. And it was also a crew change.

The helmsman yelled, "Due west! Not one quarter to the northwest! Not one quarter to the southwest!"

Mr. Niño yelled, "Due west! Not one quarter to the northwest! Not one quarter to the southwest!"

Mr. de la Cosa, of the new crew, yelled, "Due west! Not one quarter to the northwest! Not one quarter to the southwest!"

Mr. de la Cosa's helmsman yelled, "Due west! Not one quarter to the northwest! Not one quarter to the southwest!"

A black slate was kept beside the tiller. Every half-hour as the young seamen sang his chant, the helmsman or officer in charge of the watch recorded information. He confirmed that the direction dictated by Chris had been kept by constantly checking

"DUE WEST!"

the magnetic compass. In addition, he recorded his estimate of the speed of the ship. This was done by experience. There was no instrument for determining speed. The officer judged the ship's speed by glancing overboard to see how fast the ship moved past seaweed or something else floating in the sea.

Every morning, Chris took the slate into his cabin and recorded the information in his Journal of the Voyage. Then he plotted the previous day's progress on a large sheepskin map. Once again he was sailing by "dead reckoning." His course was due west and Chris did not plan on changing that course until he spotted China!

Scudding west was easy. There were no storms, no high seas, no vicious winds, just steady wind at their back pushing them over 100 miles west per day. But Chris knew seamen. Soon enough, they would realize the strong steady wind in one direction was a double-edged sword. How would they

EACH MORNING, CHRIS RECORDED THE INFORMATION

get back to Spain?

No one grumbled yet. The men seemed in very good spirits. They had spotted seaweed and even a tiny green crab in the seaweed. These they thought were signs they were already approaching land. They dropped a line with a lead weight overboard to measure the depth to bottom. The line was 1200 feet long.

"It never reached bottom!" cried one seaman. Chris remembered what old Pedro in Palos had told him about a great sea of seaweed. Each day, they saw more and more seaweed. Soon the sea was a smooth expanse of green in every direction. By the 21st of September, the seamen were alarmed. There was almost no wind. What if the ships became stuck in the seaweed?

"Look," barked Chris, as he scooped up a bucket of sea water. "The seaweed is no more than one inch thick on the top of the ocean! How could we get

"THE SEAWOOD IS NO MORE THAN ONE INCH THICK!"

stuck in such a trifle?"

"But there is no wind," blurted one seaman.

Chris had no answer for that.

The men had very little to do. The ships slowly sailed west. The men went swimming, easily keeping pace with the ships. At first, they joked with the men on the other ships. But more and more often, they shared fears with the men on the other ships. How would they ever get back to Spain?

The wind returned on September 26th. Day after day, the ships sailed farther west. Now the wind, which the men once wanted to return, became their enemy. It pushed them farther and farther from Spain.

On October 2nd, the wind blustered in a fury. The ships blazed along, averaging over 140 miles per day. The men knew they had sailed over 2000 miles. They had sailed much farther west than any crews had sailed in history.

"BUT THERE IS NO WIND"

"But who will ever know how far we sailed if we never return to civilization?" griped one sailor.

Then they lost the wind again. The ships barely moved. It was almost more than the seamen could bear. Chris could tell they were about to crack under the strain. *God help us, where is land?*

On October 9th, the captains of the two caravels, the Pinzon brothers, boarded the *Santa Maria* to talk to Chris. Their faces were stony.

Inside the cabin, Martin Pinzon didn't hide his anger. "Why must we go on? It will be difficult enough to return to Spain if we turn around this very moment, which is exactly what I intend to do!" Chris asked Vincent Pinzon, "And do you agree?"

"Yes," he said reluctantly.

So both captains wanted to turn back. Chris knew he had to compromise. He himself would have pushed on indefinitely. But that would not be possible under the circumstances. So he prayed

"WHY MUST WE GO ON?"

silently. And the answer came to him. He had a vision of Jesus walking out of the tomb, radiant and alive: the best news in the history of mankind.

He said, “Give me three more days...”

“And then you will turn back?” snarled Martin Pinzon.

“Yes. We will turn back.”

The next day the wind grew stronger. Soon the fleet skimmed along west at a dazzling speed that would take them nearly two hundred miles that day. Now the crew was openly angry because they were being pushed farther and farther from Spain. They didn’t know about their captain’s promise to the Pinzons.

The crew could not be reasoned with. If the wind was weak, as it had been the previous two days, they fumed because they were going to be stranded at the edge of the world. If the wind was strong, they fumed because they were being blown even farther

"GIVE ME THREE MORE DAYS..."

from Spain.

Chris was in his cabin praying for God's help when there was a knock on the door. "Enter!" he called out.

His first officer Juan de la Cosa entered. "Captain, the crew is close to taking over the ship..."

"Yes, I know they are close to mutiny. They want to take over the ship and turn back to Spain. This is the most dangerous day of the entire voyage. We must ask God to help us stop them."

"Perhaps if we three officers stand before them with loaded muskets..."

"No!" Chris motioned to the door. "I'll talk to them."

"It's wrong to bargain with a crew that won't follow orders."

"No crew in history has ever endured the doubts they have endured. Get them together."

Juan de la Cosa walked outside and yelled, "All

"NO! I'LL TALK TO THEM"

hands to the captain's cabin! Shake a leg!"

Chris prayed for God's help, then walked outside. God had let him stand tall and talk boldly to kings and queens. But never did he need God's help as much as he did now.

"Men," he said calmly. "I know you want to return to Spain. But what of the signs of land we've seen?"

"They all turn out to be false!" cried a seaman.

That was true. Chris knew he had to try to see it from their point of view. He said boldly, "You have traveled over open ocean farther than any crew in history. You think you have sailed into a part of the Atlantic Ocean that receives only winds from the east. You think the journey back to Spain will be difficult..."

"Or impossible!" screamed one seaman hysterically.

Chris remained calm. "Not impossible—but you

"YOU HAVE TRAVELED FARTHER THAN ANY CREW IN HISTORY"

will have to work like mules changing the sails constantly. And what if the food runs out first? What if the water runs out first?"

The crew was stunned. "You know all that?" blurted one seaman. "Then why are we sailing farther west?"

"Because I have faith in God helping our great adventure. I will make a bargain with you men. If we don't see land in two days we will turn back."

"Just two days?" asked a seaman. A grin split his face.

Suddenly, the entire crew cheered.

One seaman yelled, "Three cheers for an honest, reasonable captain!" And he said in a lower voice, "A captain who will take us back to Spain."

Chris went back inside his cabin. He felt like he had done nothing. The destiny of the voyage was in God's hands, as it had been from the beginning.

THE DESTINY OF THE VOYAGE WAS IN GOD'S HANDS

"A FLOWER!"

CHAPTER 9

A man screamed, "A flower!"

Chris ran outside his cabin. He smiled at the dawn sky. "Thanks to God for this glorious day." It was October 11th.

The entire crew gathered to gawk across at the *Niña*. A seaman on the*Niña* held up a green branch. He yelled, "Look at the red flower! I saw it floating alongside the ship."

They heard shouting from the *Pinta*. A seaman had found a stick floating in the ocean. The stick had lines carved on it!

One of the seamen beside Chris took a deep breath. "And we were so close to turning back."

The wind was still strong. They were blazing west. All day they found signs of land: more carved sticks, more pieces of land plants, kinds of birds they had never seen before.

The crew was cheerful until nightfall. Then the blazing speed and nearness of land scared them. What if they hit a reef in the night? The sea was choppier now than it had been during the entire voyage. Not many men were able to sleep.

At two o'clock in the morning, the moon beamed high above to the west. The moon was nearly full and lit up the ocean below it like a giant lantern. Dozens of anxious eyes scoured the western horizon. Where was land?

"Land! Land!" It sounded like a seaman on the *Pinta* screaming.

On the *Pinta* the cannon fired twice. That was the signal for land!

Everyone on the *Santa Maria* strained their eyes to see if it was true. It wouldn't be the first time someone had mistakenly thought they'd seen land. Suddenly, everyone seemed to recognize a white strip on the horizon. A beach! Straight ahead!

A BEACH! STRAIGHT AHEAD!

Chris yelled, "All hands, fasten down the sails!"

Seamen scrambled to lower the big sails. They had to slow their ships. Soon, all three ships were drifting to the south. They must wait until daybreak and find a place to go ashore. Each ship had seven anchors aboard. On the *Santa Maria*, Chris was ready to use all of them—even the huge plate anchor that a captain used only as a last resort. Drifting off a beach with the wind blowing into the beach was very dangerous.

Chris thought to himself, *Only God knows how many ships have hit a reef far out from the beach itself!*

The beach stretched for miles. It was a very tense night. At daybreak, Chris saw he could skirt around the land to the south. The seamen put up more sail and after about five miles of sailing west, Chris saw they could skirt the land to the north. So the land was probably an island. Waves breaking far from the

CHRIS SAW THEY COULD SKIRT THE LAND TO THE NORTH

white beach proved there was a dangerous reef surrounding the island.

Chris lead the fleet north. Five miles to the north there was a gap in the reef. The ships cruised into a beautiful bay and anchored in thirty feet of water.

Juan de la Cosa sighed. "It is October 12th, 1492. We have been at sea for thirty-three days."

"Thanks to Almighty God we found land," said Chris. "Lower the rowboat into the water."

A seaman shouted, "There are people on the beach!"

And people were on the beach. They appeared to be brown-skinned men who wore no clothes at all.

Within minutes, Chris and a few others stepped out of the rowboat into the surf and waded onto the shore. The captains of the other two ships had landed, too. Chris greeted the brown-skinned men who had watched them arrive, and then he fell to his knees.

"Thank God for bringing us here safely," he said.

"THANK GOD FOR BRINGING US HERE SAFELY"

"I name this island San Salvador for our Holy Savior."

The men of the fleet carried a huge, white banner with a green cross. It represented the holy reign of King Ferdinand and Queen Isabella of Spain.

Chris tried to talk to the brown-skinned men. They were all young men, muscular, and trim. Straight black hair fell down in bangs over eyes that reminded Chris of the people Marco Polo had written about who lived in China and Japan. Chris knew Marco Polo had written of islands near China and Japan. They were called the "Indies."

"Surely, you men must be 'Indians,'" said Chris.

It was quickly apparent the brown-skinned men spoke a language completely unlike any language the men in the fleet had heard before. And the men had been to many countries and knew many languages. They were able to speak to the "Indians" only with signs.

"SURELY, YOU MEN MUST BE 'INDIANS' "

The "Indians" wore nosepieces with tiny pieces of gold in them. Chris touched a tiny chunk of gold in a nosepiece on one of the men and gave the group of "Indians" a questioning look. The brown-skinned "Indians" waved toward the western horizon. With artful gestures they soon explained the gold was found on another island.

"Japan!" exclaimed Martin Pinzon. "That's where the gold will be found."

Chris did not want to look for gold. But he knew he must. He had to take jewels or silver or gold back to Spain to reward the men who had paid for his voyage. And the promise of more gold would guarantee future voyages. Without treasure, many in Spain would call his voyage a failure.

Over the next two days, Chris learned the "Indians" were very trusting. No weapons were seen except tiny darts they used to kill birds and small animals for food. Their homes were wood frames

GOLD WAS FOUND ON ANOTHER ISLAND

covered with huge palm leaves. They farmed corn and yams. They made bread from the yucca plant. They spun cotton and wove cloth. They made pots from clay. From tall, hardwood trees, they hollowed out canoes so large, they held forty men.

Chris felt sad as he said good-bye to the natives. They were so trusting and so defenseless. Somehow, he must try to protect them.

Over the next several weeks the ships discovered island after island. Chris named one of them after Ferdinand and another after Isabella. He even named one for their son Prince Juan. The men in the fleet now called him "Admiral." Several told him they were sorry for ever doubting him. But some officers held back their gratitude.

Martin Pinzon grumbled, "After all, we haven't found gold yet!"

They spent many days on the huge island called Cuba. Despite rumors of gold here and there among

"AFTER ALL, WE HAVEN'T FOUND GOLD YET!"

the Indians, they found very little except in the ornaments the Indians already had somehow obtained. Were the Indians not telling them where it was?

On November 22nd, Martin Pinzon disappeared with the *Pinta*. Chris knew he was the most impatient of all to find gold. Pinzon had simply gone off on his own to look for it. Pinzon had said more than once Chris wasted too much of their precious time being nice to the Indians.

Finally, Chris and his men explored the island of Haiti. On Christmas day, the *Santa Maria* went aground during the watch of Juan de la Cosa. The waves drove the ship higher and higher onto a coral reef. Finally, the ship could not take the strain. It began to break apart. The men managed to save most of their supplies by taking them ashore in rowboats.

Gold began to appear all over. There was no

IT BEGAN TO BREAK APART

doubt some major source of gold existed on the island. Chris could not find it though, so he traded beads and trinkets for gold. He had to have enough gold when he returned to Spain to make people want to pay for another voyage.

"God has struck a bargain!" he exclaimed one day. He was sure of it. The wreck of the *Santa Maria* was God's will. No one was injured. Suddenly, they found gold everywhere.

He had another thought. Did God intend for some of them to stay here in this new land?

Chris prayed for God's answer. He had prayed very hard every day of his life. And he had been very blessed. Sometimes he prayed so hard on the ship, the men had a difficult time getting his attention. He didn't think that was unusual at all.

God was silent this time. Chris used his reason. It would be very hard for the *Niña* to carry sixty-five men and enough supplies for that many men back to

GOD WAS SILENT THIS TIME

Spain. It was going to be a very difficult voyage into the easterly winds. So Chris ordered the men to take the timbers of the wrecked *Santa Maria* and use them to build a fort. He picked forty men to stay behind at the fort. Most of them wanted to stay. They felt like they were first in line for what was going to be great riches for everyone.

"I christen the fort Navidad!" said Chris. "Navidad" was Spanish for Christmas day, the day the *Santa Maria* broke apart.

Suddenly, Martin Pinzon arrived with the *Pinta*. He acted as if nothing had happened. Chris was extremely angry. In his mind, Martin Pinzon had deserted the fleet. Martin Pinzon only came back because he had heard about the gold.

Vincent Pinzon stood by his brother. Chris didn't hold it against him. He knew how loyal brothers were to each other. He thought about Bart all the time. One of his biggest regrets about the voyage

CHRIS WAS EXTREMELY ANGRY

was that Bart wasn't there with him.

Chris swallowed his anger and remained silent about Martin Pinzon's disloyalty to him, the admiral of the fleet. He wanted the Pinta to sail back to Spain next to the *Niña*. A voyage with two ships was many times safer for all the officers and seamen than a voyage with one lone ship. Several Indians had been persuaded to go back to Spain with them, too.

On January 16, 1493, three hours before dawn, the sails of the *Niña* and the *Pinta* caught the ocean winds and drifted away from Navidad.

At the helm of the *Niña*, Juan de la Cosa's forehead was creased with worry...

THE SAILS OF THE *NINA* AND THE *PINTA* CAUGHT THE WIND

HAD GOD EVER FAILED HIM?

CHAPTER 10

All the officers on the *Pinta* and the *Niña* worried.

Martin Pinzon's loud complaint still echoed: "What if Columbus is mistaken about our location by many hundreds of miles? Will we ever find Spain?"

The officers knew only too well how many mistakes the Admiral could have made plotting their location on his maps as they jogged in and out of the many islands. Now they were sailing for Spain and they had no choice but to assume the location Chris had plotted for Navidad was correct.

Chris knew how tricky navigation was, but he was not worried. He trusted God. Had God ever failed him?

It was not as if Chris didn't have a plan based on reason and experience. He knew God did not want his faithful servants to be fools. Chris' plan was based on his many voyages all around the Atlantic Ocean. He knew that the tradewinds scurried a ship along to the west if one sailed far enough south. And he also knew if one sailed far enough north the winds blew in the opposite direction. The "westerlies," as they were called, scurried a ship along to the east.

"Northeast, Mr. de la Cosa!" ordered Chris.

Within minutes Juan de la Cosa had the *Niña* sailing northeast. The *Pinta* followed.

Sailing northeast was almost as difficult as sailing straight east. The ships had to constantly tack back and forth. The crews were quickly exhausted changing the sails. Food was in short supply. Nothing was left but bread and the occasional fish they caught.

After 16 days, they had not sailed even a third of the way back to Spain. The crews were gaunt and tired. They grumbled over their poor diet. Would they have the strength to sail all the way back to Spain?

"NORTHEAST, MR. DE LA COSTA!"

Hours a day, Chris prayed to God for help.

On the first morning of February, 1493, he stepped outside his cabin. His voice choked with gratitude, "Thanks to God for His heavenly wind!"

The wind had shifted. It blew from the west!

Chris changed their course to straight east. The two ships scudded before the powerful westerlies Chris had predicted. The wind became stronger and stronger. Not one man on the ships remembered ever sailing faster. They sailed 200 miles on February 5th.

And they blazed east day after day.

One evening, the sky gave Chris a sick feeling. He had a gift for understanding weather. This time he prayed he was not right. But at dawn on the 12th of February, they sailed into a storm. Chris knew it was going to be the worst storm of his long life at sea!

Both ships dropped all sails. The masts were

THEY BLAZED EAST DAY AFTER DAY

bare. The ships bounced on ferocious waves—hour after hour. Cargo on deck shifted treacherously. Rain raked the ships. Jagged lightning popped all around and scorched the sea.

Chris had no idea if the *Pinta* had sunk or not. He prayed. After forty-eight hours of the monster storm, he began to think maybe God would not save him this time. How long would it be before one of the colossal waves caught the *Niña* just right and turned it over? Sometimes God did not save good people. Chris remembered only too well how suddenly his precious Felipa had died. God had His own mysterious plans for men and women.

Chris wrote a brief history of the voyage, sealed it inside an empty barrel and had the barrel thrown overboard. If both ships went to the bottom of the ocean maybe someday someone would find the barrel and know what had happened to his brave men.

FORTY EIGHT HOURS OF THE MONSTER STORM

He felt better after that.

"We are in God's hands now," he told Juan de la Cosa. "His will be done."

It was almost sunset on the 14th of February. The storm had battered the *Niña* for sixty hours!

Suddenly, they sailed out of the storm!

They had reached the islands called the Azores. They were back in familiar waters. The *Pinta* was nowhere to be seen. Had it gone to the bottom of the ocean in the storm? Chris wanted to stop in the Azores and get supplies. But the Portuguese were hostile to a ship flying the flag of Spain. They even tried to arrest Chris. The *Niña* escaped to sail on toward Spain.

And 250 miles away from the Azores the *Niña* hit another violent storm that drove it not to Spain—but straight to Portugal. There a Portuguese warship stopped it. None other than Dias, the great captain who sailed to the southern tip of Africa,

"HIS WILL BE DONE"

boarded the *Niña*. Dias glared angrily at Chris, but he listened to what Chris had accomplished since August, 1492.

"Glory to God!" said Dias finally. He broke into a grin. "You are truly the greatest Admiral of the oceans!"

Dias took Chris to King John. The king was unfriendly. Surely, such a wild tale could not be true. Chris brought the Indians from the *Niña* to meet the king. Chris explained the voyage again and again.

The king began to accept his story as true, but he grew angrier and angrier. This new sea route and its wealth should have been Portugal's! Chris had brought the proposal to him first. King John would be remembered throughout history as the king who turned down Columbus. He dismissed Chris as if he would not be able to control his terrible anger much longer.

"GLORY TO GOD!"

Once again the *Niña* went to sea. By April, the ship anchored safely in Palos in Spain. Chris went ashore first to see his son, Diego. Then he waited to see the king and queen. Chris was a celebrity. Everyone in Palos seemed to know of his great feat. Chris asked about the old man Pedro who had been so helpful to Chris before the fleet had left Spain on the great voyage. What he found out made him very sad. The old man—named Pedro Vasquez—was dead. No one knew who had murdered him.

"God help me! I'll bet Martin Pinzon had something to do with it!"

"He is dead, too," said a man who lived in Palos.

Chris learned Martin Pinzon had arrived before him with the *Pinta*. Pinzon had tried desperately to get an audience with the king and queen but they had refused to see him. Exhausted by fighting storms and hearing his king and queen regarded him as a traitorous fool, Pinzon had gone to his home in Palos

CHRIS WENT ASHORE FIRST TO SEE HIS SON, DIEGO

and had died within days.

Some urged Chris to punish Vincent Pinzon. Some wanted him to bring charges against Juan de la Cosa for allowing the *Santa Maria* to run aground. Other men had made mistakes on the voyage, too. Many had openly opposed him. Chris had influence with the king and queen now. Why not have these bad men punished?

Chris was not interested in revenge. On Judgment Day, God would punish these men if they were sinful.

Finally, the king and queen called for Chris.

When he arrived at the royal court Queen Isabella told him, "We are delighted with you. You are now officially our Admiral of the Oceans. You are governor of all the land you discovered. You have gold and fame. What more could any man want?"

Chris was surprised. "Why, I must sail the ocean again!"

And thanks to God he did.

"I MUST SAIL THE OCEANS AGAIN!"